P9-AFU-875

PS3537
T323
B7

20771

TERTELING LIBRARY
THE COLLEGE OF IDAHO
CALDWELL, IDAHO

ARY

Brewsie and Willie

GERTRUDE STEIN

Brewsie

AND

Willie

RANDOM HOUSE · NEW YORK

SECOND PRINTING

PS 3537
T 323
B 7

2 0771

Copyright, 1946, by Random House, Inc.

*Published simultaneously in Canada by
Random House of Canada Limited*

Manufactured in the United States of America

Designer: Ernst Reichl

STRAHORN LIBRARY
COLLEGE OF IDAHO

Brewsie and Willie

CHAPTER

One

YOU KNOW WILLIE, said Brewsie, I think we are all funny, pretty funny, about this fraternisation business, now just listen. They did not have to make any anti-fraternisation ruling for the German army in France because although the Germans did their best to fraternise, no French woman would look or speak to them or recognise their existence. I kind of wonder would our women be like French or be like Germans, if the horrible happened and our country was conquered and occupied.

Willie: Well I wouldnt want any American woman to be like a Frenchwoman.

Brewsie: No you would want them to be like the Germans, sleep with the conquerors.

Willie: You get the hell out of here, Brewsie. No American woman would sleep with a foreigner.

Brewsie: But you admire the Germans who do. Which do you want American women to be like.

Willie: I know what I dont want them to be

like, I dont want them to be like any lousy foreigner.

Brewsie: But all your fathers and mothers were lousy foreigners.

Willie: You get the hell out of here, Brewsie. What's that to you, I am going to sleep with any German wench who'll sleep with me and they all will.

Brewsie: Sure they all will but all the same if the horrible happened and our country was defeated and occupied, how about it.

Willie: Well our country isnt going to be defeated and occupied, that's all there is to that.

Brewsie: Yes but you never can tell in a war.

Willie: And that's the reason there aint going to be any more war not if I can help it.

Brewsie: But if you cant help it.

Willie: I'll see to it that I do help it, there aint going to be any more war.

Brewsie: But that's what they said last time and hell here we are.

Willie: Well did I say we werent here, we're here all right, you betcha we're here, and I am going to sleep with any German girl who'll sleep with me, and they all will and that's what I call fraternisation, and they let us do it and we're doing it.

4

Brewsie: But Willie listen.

Willie: Aint I listening, aint I always listening, you're always talking and I am always listening.

Brewsie: Well anyway, Willie, just listen.

While Brewsie talked, it was not alone Willie who sometimes listened, there were others more or less listening, Jo, and Bob and Ralph and Don and there was Brock, he was older, he liked to talk about how his father and mother moved from one house to another and what illnesses they had had and what it did to them and what flowers his mother grew and that she was fond of cooking and eating, and that he was not the only child but they did like him that is to say he was interested in everything they wrote to him and was natural enough because although he had been married, he did not know whether he was married now or not, anyway he did listen to Brewsie, because Brewsie was really very interesting and had a lot to say that was interesting and he, whenever he Brock had time, he did listen to him, he was a good chap Brewsie and had a lot to say that was really interesting.

Listen, said Brewsie, listen to me. I want to know why do you fellows feel the way you do.

Jo: Oh go way Brewsie, dont you know we're

disillusioned, that's what we are, disillusioned, that's the word, aint it, fellows, disillusioned.

All of 'em: Sure, that's the word, disillusioned.

Brock: No no I am not disillusioned, as long as my mother is fond of flowers, and she is and fond of cooking as she is and fond of eating as she is, and likes to move into other houses which she does I could never be that word I could never be disillusioned. No, Jo, no, no no, and I think you all know I mean it I do I never could be disillusioned.

Willie: Take me away, that man makes me crazy. I just cant stand another minute of it, take me away.

Brewsie: All right, Willie, let's go. Come along, Jo.

Jo: Yes I got to go to the river to wait on a girl.

Brewsie: Where is she.

Jo: She is gone home to eat but I said I'd sit on the river bank and wait and I'm going to, want to come along.

Willie: There aint two.

Jo: No there aint but one, want to come along.

Brewsie: Let's all three go.

Jo: That's all right with me.

Look, said Willie, there comes a man-eating dog.

It was a dark day but it did not rain. The dog was white and gentle. That is what Willie said.

6

Brewsie does talk to himself, he said to himself, how can I be interested in how many people will be killed or how much property will be destroyed in the next war, how many people will be killed in the next war.

They went on to the river. It is not always easy to sail a sailboat up a river.

That made them talk about what they did remember, steering an airplane. Some of them sighed, it made them sigh because they liked it. It was like sleeping in a bed, it made them sigh, it did make them sigh because they liked it.

I remember, he said, he said, I remember.

They saw three others coming along, one of them said, what we doing just walking, aint anybody going to buy anything.

Brewsie remembered about buying, there was a time when anybody could buy something that is if he had money with him. Brewsie said that spending money if you had it, well it was just spending money and spending money was not only easy as anything it was more than anything.

I know what you mean, said Willie.

I do too, said Jo, let's go buy something. We aint found anything to buy for the kind of money we got, said Willie, and then the girl came along. If you put your arm all over a girl, well any girl does any girl say, tell him I dont want him, but no girls do because there is chewing gum and tobacco and coffee and chocolate, yes there is. Does, said Brewsie, does any one want to buy anything if it can be given to them, if they can get it without buying. Nobody answered him, they were busy other ways.

It's a long war but it will end, said Brewsie, and then we will go home. Where's home, said a man just behind him.

What's your name, said Brewsie.

Paul is my name and if it aint Paul it's Donald, what do you want with my name.

I want to know how old you are and where you come from.

Oh get the hell out of here, said Donald Paul and then he sat down.

Let's, said Donald Paul, let's talk about beds. What kind of beds, said Brewsie. Oh any kind, the kind you sleep in, the kind you make for yourselves and the kind others make for you. A bed is a bed, just write that down if you know how to read and write, a bed's a bed. When you wish you were dead you always wish for a bed. Yes that's the way it is. Remember you know when they put you in prison they make you make your own bed. I just read about it this evening. Yes, said Brewsie, if there is a bed. Yeah you're right too, if there is a bed. And they both sighed not loud, not really at all. Anybody knows how long a day is when evening comes. They gather that they had rather not be able to sit than not.

Yes, said Brewsie, do be anxious.

It was almost as much aloud as that.

Donald Paul snorted.

Allowed, he said, allowed, what's allowed, anything that is allowed is just what they never said. There are, said Donald Paul, yes there are, said Brewsie. Are what, said Willie. Eight million unemployed any next year, said Jo. Oh go to hell out of here, said Willie and as he spoke he fell asleep just like that.

Two

Brewsie

I'm here

What you doing.

I'm thinking.

I am thinking about religion.

What religion.

Well Willie's, somebody said to me today why don't the G.I.'s have the Bible around like the doughboys did, why aint there ever a Bible in a plane.

Why should there be, there aint anything the matter with the plane.

Of course there could be.

Ya but if there could be it would be the fault of the ground men, and if there is any flack then you're taught how to dive in so that it dont hit you and if you dont do it right it does and anyway there is of course there is the calculation of errors.

What's the matter with you Brewsie, dont you know all that.

Yes it is kind of funny I know all that, they do say though that the doughboys always had Bibles around, that's what they say.

Well, said Jo, why do you worry.

I don't worry, said Brewsie, I never worry I am kind of foggy in the head and I want to be clear, that's all.

Willie: Well you never will, you just keep on thinking and talking the more foggy you feel. Now you take us, we dont think we know that all America is just so and we are all Americans, that's what we are all Americans.

Brewsie: I wish I was a girl if I was a girl I would be a WAC and if I was a WAC, oh my Lord, just think of that.

Don: Dont you go being funny Brewsie, I been out with a WAC, yes I have, well no she was not an officer WAC although I have been out even with an officer WAC, how can you worry when anything is like that.

Brewsie: Well now boys let's all get together and think.

Willie: All right now how would you want us to get together and think.

11

Brewsie: Well let's think about how everybody perhaps will get killed in the next war.

Willie: Well they sure will if they fight the war good enough. If you fight a war good enough everybody ought to get killed.

Brewsie: You mean the other side.

Willie: No not the other side, that's only when one side fights good enough, but when they both do, and that can happen too, well when they both do, then everybody will be dead, all dead, fine, then nobody's got to worry about jobs.

Brewsie: But oh dear me, there are the wives and children. Yes there are.

Brock: You know the other day I heard a colored major say, he had no children although he was married nine years and I said, how is that, and he said, is this America any place to make born a Negro child.

Willie: I dont want to hear any talk like that, you know right well Brock I dont want to hear any talk like that.

But Willie, said Brock, Willie you listen to Brewsie and he talks like that and when I talk like Brewsie talks you tell me you dont want me to talk at all like that, that's not right Willie, that's not right, it is not right, Willie, it is not right.

Willie: Oh my God.

While they were talking they did not know what country they were in. If they did know they might talk about it but they did not know what country they were in, and little by little they knew less what country they were in. It was not night yet, it was not even late in the afternoon, they knew that, and sometimes they thought about that, but Brewsie did not talk about that so they did not have to listen about that not that afternoon.

It was early in the morning, and there was anybody there, they never thought that there was anybody there even when there was.

Let's go and have a drink, said Willie, but they could get a drink where they were so they did not go and get a drink, they had a drink where they were.

I was in a hotel, said Willie, and I saw from the window around the corner somebody getting into bed and I could not tell whether it was a little girl or a little woman.

What time was it, said Brewsie.

About half past ten, said Willie.

You couldnt tell by that, said Brewsie, not by that. A little girl could be going to bed then, yes she could.

I know, said Willie, I know, it might have been a little girl and it might have been a round-faced little woman, I kind of think it was a round-faced little woman and I couldnt tell whether she was kneeling to say her prayers or to take make-up off her face, I just couldnt tell.

Was there a mirror in front of her, said Brewsie.

I just couldnt tell, said Willie.

Even a little woman could kneel and say her prayers as well as a little girl, said Brewsie.

Could she, said Willie.

Yes she could, said Brewsie.

Well I dont know, said Willie, it was so around the corner.

Well couldnt you see her the next day.

I tell you it was the back of a house around the corner, how could I tell which house it was next day.

Well, said Brewsie, why didnt you go around that night and see.

I tell you, said Willie, it was around the corner and the front wouldnt be the same as the back.

Well couldnt you count, said Jo waking up.

No not in French how could you count in French around the corner with the back and the front different and not sure it was a girl or a little woman. No I just never did find out.

Well why didnt you go back to the hotel and try again, said Brewsie, try to see her get to bed again.

14

Because I never have gone back there, said Willie, I never have and when I do get back she will be gone sure she will.

Nobody ever moves in France, said Jo.

No, maybe though it was a hotel.

Well if it was, said Brewsie, it was not a little girl.

I guess you're right Brewsie, I guess it was a little woman, a little round-faced woman and she was taking off her make-up.

Perhaps, said Brewsie, it was a little round-faced woman and she was saying her prayers.

Not likely, said Willie.

Three

BREWSIE: Are we isolationists or are we isolated, are we efficient or are we quick to make up for long preparation, if we were caught without time to get it all in order would we be ready, would we be, well did we be, if Japan had followed up, oh dear me, said Brewsie, oh dear me, are we efficient or are we slow and so we are very quick to make up for being slow, oh dear me, said Brewsie, and do we like the German girls best because we are virgins and they do all the work.

Willie: You get the hell out of here Brewsie, I am no virgin, I never was a virgin, I never will be a virgin.

No, said Brewsie, no, you never were a virgin, well then you dont know the difference perhaps you still are a virgin.

Jo: That sounds funny, Brewsie, that's not the

16

way you talk, Brewsie, what's the matter with you, Brewsie.

Brewsie: I dont know, I kind of feel funny, it is true over half the E. T. O. are virgins, they are they are, and that's why they like the German girls I get so mad I just have to say it, I just get so mad.

Willie: Well I get mad too, if you say I am a virgin.

Jo: Well, Willie, perhaps you are. Brewsie is right, a whole lot of the army are virgins. I dont say they cant but they dont and that's the reason they got to have so many pin-ups and German girls, yes sometimes I guess Brewsie is right, you just bellow, Willie, you just bellow and Brewsie is just foggy so he is but I know, I never say it but I know, a lot of us is just virgins, Willie, just E. T. O. virgins, Willie, all you fellows, are you or are you not E. T. O. Virgins.

Willie: You get the hell out of here, Jo, I can stand what Brewsie says but I wont stand anything you say, I just wont and I warn you right here and now if you call me a virgin again some night or some day you'll die and it wont be any enemy that will have killed you, it will have been just me.

Brock: Oh boys, boys, listen to me, I am older than any of you and I dont know whether I am married or not and I am always interested in what my mother does and I do like to drink but nobody ever thinks of calling me a virgin. You wouldnt, Willie, and you wouldnt, Jo, and you wouldnt, Brewsie, you never would think of calling me a virgin. So dont you be worried, Willie, dont you be worried, you just listen to me and dont you be worried.

Willie: Oh.

Brewsie: But to come back to what is worrying me, to come back to it, are we isolationists or are we isolated.

Willie: You just want to explain, Brewsie, so go ahead, you will anyway so go ahead, we just listen anyway, so just go ahead. Come on, Jo, come on, everybody, Brewsie is thinking.

Brewsie: Well I just am thinking are we isolationists or are we isolated.

Jo: Well what about it.

Well you see, said Brewsie, I kind of like to be liked. Willie likes to be liked, so do you all, well yes I do like to be liked, I just could cry if they dont like me, yes I could. I do like to be liked.

And besides, said Jo, it's dangerous not to be liked, if Willie did not like me I would just be scared.

Brock: I am sure everybody does like me, I do I am sure I do what makes anyone like me.

Oh my God, said Willie, take me away.

All right, said Brewsie, all right where shall we go.

Right back where we started from, said Willie. And the flowers.

Oh come along, said Jo, Brewsie will remember what he wants to say for another day.

No, said Brewsie, I wont remember but I will find it out again.

Let's go, said Willie.

And they went.

The sun was shining and they were all worried, there was nothing to worry about, the sun was shining and they were all worried.

It used to be fine, said Willie, before the war when we used to believe what the newspapers and the magazines said, we used to believe them when we read them and now when it's us they write about we know it's lies, just lies, just bunches of lies, and if it's just bunches of lies, what we going to read when we get home, answer me that, Brewsie, answer me that.

I saw a girl, said Donald Paul, she was saying how can I replace potatoes, how can I take the place of potatoes. My darling, I said, you just cant. Brewsie: I am going to begin to talk and I am just going on talking, that's what I am going to do.

Sure you are, said Willie.

I say, said Brewsie, and I am just going to be solemn, just as solemn as anything, are we isolationists or are we isolated, do we like Germans because we are greedy and callous like them. Oh dear, I guess you boys better go away, I might just begin to cry and I'd better be alone. I am a G. I. and perhaps we better all cry, it might do us good crying sometimes does.

Oh get the hell out of here, Brewsie, said Willie.

Crying does good, said Jo, but I dont like it, not anybody's crying.

Where is Donald Paul, said Brewsie.

I told him to go away, said Willie.

If they knew it was Sunday afternoon then it was Sunday afternoon, nicely and quietly Sunday afternoon. Even yesterday was Sunday afternoon, Brewsie said so and they all said, yes, yesterday even yesterday was Sunday afternoon too.

Two majors came along, one was a fat major and one was a thin major, they were in transport, the fat major said, I wonder when we get home, can we make them see that it is just as good not to work seven days a week all day, that railroads get along just as well if you go home for a day and a half a week and work in your garden. The thin major said, I wonder, no I dont wonder about the railroads getting along just as good, I wonder if they'll see it and let us take a day and a half off and perhaps longer and a month for a vacation like they do over here, I wonder. And do you suppose, said the fat major we could retire when we were fifty instead of when we were seventy. I wonder, said the thin major and they went home in the twilight, a nice twilight.

Brewsie when he was awake woke slowly, it was just as well as when he went to sleep, he went to sleep slowly.

Willie never asked him why, Willie knew why.

Said Brewsie, do you remember, Willie, what I was talking about. Well I do, I was talking about a lot of things and I was going to talk a long time and I was going to commence with, Are we isolationists or are we isolated.

Two Red Cross nurses came along, they were lieutenants still they did say, listen he sounds interesting. Tell me, said the fatter and younger, dont you think it is awful that the French have no leaders.

Havent they, said Donald Paul, and if they have why do they want them, a leader is some one who leads you where you dont want to go, where do you want to go, sister, can I lead you.

The older and the thinner said, we were not talking to you, we were talking to him, he sounds interesting.

Donald Paul: Fair sister, you are right, he not only sounds interesting but he is interesting.

Brewsie: I have a great deal to say.

The older one: Yes, that is why we are listening.

Brewsie: If I have a great deal to say it will take a long time to say it.

Yes, said the younger, but how can the French expect to come back if they have no leaders.

Why why why, how how how, said Donald Paul.

How, said Jo, I dont know how.

The older: Yes but he does, you tell us, she said to Brewsie.

Brewsie, said yes, I'll tell you. Leaders, what are leaders, yes was right, a leader either does not lead you or if he does he leads you where you do not want to go. Isnt it so, sisters, isnt it, where do you want to go, where do the French want to go, they dont want to go anywhere, they want enough to eat, a place to sleep, and fuel to keep them warm, that's what they want, leaders never give you that, they kind of scratch around and get it for themselves. No he is right what can leaders do, we always have leaders but where do they lead us. No listen to me and I will tell you about efficiency and about being isolated and why although rich we are poor and why although quick we are slow and how, well leaders better stay at home a while and lead everybody that way.

Chorus of a crowd: Ah yes, let's go home, I want to go home, we want to go home, everybody wants to go home. And then somebody began to sing Home Sweet Home.

Then everybody got quiet.

Do you know, said Donald Paul, I watch all those men all that army going around excursioning in auto-buses, so fat, so well dressed, so taken care of, and I say to myself, they want to go home and I say to myself, do they, and I say to myself, let's go home, and I say to myself, where is home, where you got a bellyful, that's home, where you got no cares, that's home.

Willie: Get the hell out of here, home is home, home is where you come from, that's home, that's fine, that's home.

Jo: You got no imagination, Willie.

Willie: To hell with imagination, I want to go home.

Yes, said the two nurses, you all want to go home, yeah you're all going home.

Yes we all are going home, home, that's where we're going, home.

Donald Paul: All too soon.

Willie: You get the hell out of here. If anybody is going to talk it's Brewsie, Brewsie, you talk.

Brewsie: Not today Willie, not today, I kind of dont understand anything today, I kind of thought I understand everything today, but today I kind of think I dont understand anything today. I aint no leader today, I'm kind of scared of being a leader today.

Willie: Ah you're no leader, Brewsie, you just talk.

Donald Paul: And what do leaders do.

Jo: They talk too, but they talk differently. Orientation, that's the word, said Donald Paul.

Now tell me, said the two nurses, do you all talk like this every day?

Not every day, said Jo.

Mostly every day, said Willie.

I think we will come again, said the younger fatter nurse and the older thinner one was very interested and they went away.

CHAPTER

Four

Jo SAID, what do you think, one of those frog girls said, I showed 'em a picture of my wife and the baby in the baby carriage and she said, what, do you have those old fashioned baby-carriages with high wheels and a baby can fall out, no we French people, we have up-to-date baby-carriages, streamlined, she said. It's funny but that's what she said, and I said, take me show me and show me she did. The town was lousy with them, sure and we never noticed, nice deep baby-carriages with low rubber-tired wheels, just as comfortable and safe as anything. Why, said that frog girl, we just use the kind of baby-carriages you have to carry packages around, not babies, never babies. Now can you beat it.

It's funny, said Willie, some ways you do and some ways you dont, it is funny, said Willie.

Jo: Let's go home and work, I want to buy one

of those up-to-date baby-carriages, I cant have no frog girl pull one like that over me.

Work, said Brewsie, yes, you know I often think American men work funny, they write to me from home, they have worked so hard they never do want to work that hard again.

Perhaps, said Donald Paul sourly, perhaps they wont have the chance.

What you mean, said Jo.

Well how about it, any work to go back to, you.

Just as much as you, said Jo. Not so, said Donald Paul. I am the only one of the whole lot of you that dont have to look for work. Why, said Jo, are you rich. Too rich to work, said Donald Paul. I, said Brock, can always find work. You certainly can, said Willie, they give you work to shut you up. But, said Brock, I can always explain things while I am working, that's it, said Willie, suppose you stopped explaining and began working anybody would drop down dead and so they got to keep you working to keep themselves from being dead.

Well anyway, said Brewsie, I often think we soldiers complain, and we complain about what the officers have but we dont complain how we have everything civilians dont have. Civilians, oh hell, what you mean Brewsie. Well dont we have food and clothes and shoes and free parties all the time, they take us everywhere, and eats, and treats, and free everything, subways and theatres and everything and my gracious, my good gracious and no worries. Oh my good gracious, oh my good gracious and no worries, my good gracious. I just could kind of just cry when I think we all got to scratch around and worry, worry and scratch around, and then those bills, pay everything on the installment plan, and coming in and coming in, oh dear, sometimes I just burst out crying in my sleep, I am older than you boys, you dont know, I could just burst out crying.

Oh, said Willie, if we got to cry let's cry into liquor, come along, which they did.

It was late afternoon and the streets were narrow and three Negro soldiers came along, there was a very little girl and her mother, one of the Negroes fell on his knee like a cavalier before the little girl and took her hand, the mother went on and then stood slightly flushed looking at her little girl, the little girl a little flushed shook the hand of the kneeling soldier, he said a word in French, she answered him, she was a very little girl, only five years old, the other two had gone on, he rose from his knee and he went on, the little girl went along with her mother.

Five

IT'S FUNNY, said Willie, the way a nigger always finds some little nigger children to talk to, you'd think there were no niggers anywhere and there he is, he just is sitting on a chair in a garden and two darky little boys talking to him and they talking French and he talking and they go on talking French and he does talk the same to them, and I do think it is funny.

Yes I found three of them taking a little nigger girl out walking and they said they had borrowed her from her mother and there they were just out walking, it is funny. Yes, said Jo, and I saw that girl in the house around the corner, she was not a little girl she was a kind of a big girl and she was reading a book and she had her elbows on the table and her head in her hands, and she was studying in a book, and she had other books on the table and she was brunette and yes, she had books. And did she see you, said Willie. Well I dont know, said Jo, but I guess she did kind of see me. And how did you know she was the same girl, well she was in the same room and there wasnt two of them so she must have been the one, you never can tell and she was not round-faced and she was not small and she was a brunette, one of those dark-complected ones but it was she all right, and she knew me even if she did not see me, not that other time, anyway. Oh forget it, said Willie, I was the one saw her. Oh well perhaps this was another place and around another corner. There is no other place, said Willie and she is my girl. Well take her if you want to, said Jo. You know, said Brewsie.

Do you fellows, have you fellows been listening. No, said Willie, we have been talking. Well, said Brewsie, I was talking to Donald Paul. Oh that fellow, said Willie, Brewsie, yes he said he wanted to. He's married. Well, said Jo, aint we all married, werent we just forgetting about being married, yes of course, yes I know about being married, well that is what I say, Donald Paul, said he wanted the government to take over everything. And, said Willie, I hope you answered him back that the first thing they the government ought to take over is this blamed army, if they manage other things the way they manage this, then they better had keep their hand off, that's all I got to say, keep their hand off. Government, aint the government back of this army, aint this a most wasteful badly managed piece of machinery, aint we all no good. Answer me that, government, answer me that, those business sharks that cant give us a job, they're bad, the government and this army, my God, we cant take care of ourselves without the government and those rich guys. I tell you boys there aint any answer, just you believe me, there aint any answer, and anybody says there is, you Brewsie, and that lousy Donald Paul, I just tell you and though I dont sound like it I've got plenty of sense, there aint any answer, there aint going to be any answer, there never has been any answer, that's the answer. Listen to me, that's the answer. There aint any answer, and we all know there aint any answer, there aint one of us in our miserable little hearts who dont know that there isnt any answer, and anybody who talks different knows he is lying, he knows darn well that that is the answer, the answer is there aint, there completely is no answer. You all listen to me you all want to go home, well you all going to be home and I tell you you'll know there just like you knew here, there aint going to be any answer.

C H A P T E R

Six

WHEN I GET HOME, said Richard, I got a home to go to, my wife and I have bought two hundred acres, we built a shack and outhouses. We got a neighbor a Pole farmer, they take care of it when we are away. My wife teaches school, and we are claiming back the land and there are rattlesnakes, so I guess it's a good place to grow grapes and make wine and what they call marc, which is a brandy, and I got a place to go home to, to hell with jobs, I got a place to go home to, and sure they will offer me a job because I dont need it, they wont offer it to those that need it, you see, I'm going home to a home. You see, where I can live, and you see I have got a home to go home to where I can live, God it's good to live, and I got a home where I can live.

I dont see why, said Ed, everybody is so scared, nothing to be scared about, my brother lived through the depression and he always had a job, and I have always been educated and I always can get well paid. What you all scared about, I am a strong man, not so strong but strong enough and now I'll tell you just how I do it, just how old I am, just what I have done, just what I am going to do, I am just going to tell you.

Willie: Oh Brewsie, kill him.

Brewsie: No Willie, you just listen.

Willie: Thank God he's dead, did you see him die, Brewsie, he died just like one of those things that go out. Oh it's fine to see them die just fine.

Are you sure he's dead, Brewsie, I am sure but are you sure he's dead.

Jo: Well you always listen to Brewsie.

Willie: Sure I listen to Brewsie. Brewsie is so earnest, and he is so careful of what he says, and besides you dont have to listen, you know what he says is so true you just dont have to listen and that's just fine, you just dont have to listen.

Brewsie: Well this time you got to listen because I've got it all doped out.

Say Brewsie, said Willie, do you know why that funny girl she says her name is Betty, but why any girl who talks no English can have a name Betty well that gets me, but besides her name being Betty, she just kind of giggles and laughs every time she sees me and not because she loves me, I can see that, but because she thinks I am ridiculous. Now why, Brewsie, why does she think I am so funny, she aint interested in me. What makes her giggle like that. Well does she do that with others, I dont know, Brewsie, she makes me so mad I just dont know. Well I know, said Jo, she thinks everybody is funny and she thinks she's funny and she's religious and I always have noticed that when anybody gets religious they giggle. What you mean, said Willie. Well I just have noticed that, said Jo, but anyway forget it, tell me something, anybody tell me something, if it is true and it is that now we have less iron ore left in our country than Canada has, why we going to go home to jobs just to use up just what we have of iron ore making gadgets to be sold on the installment plan to people worried to death because they have to pay something every month and they'd be lots happier without it, now tell me why we all want to rush home to work at a job just so our children and our children's children wont have no iron ore and be just like those European people without no iron ore. That, said Donald Paul that is what you call a high standard of living. Hell of a high standard of living, said Jo, which is on top of you all the whole time. I want to be on top of a standard of living not have it on top of me, all the time, and they say in the papers we are going to have a higher standard of living when we get home, how many more installment plans does that mean fuss and worry. It aint that, said Willie, it aint that we aint like those lousy Europeans, we like to work. Sure, said Jo, but isnt there any other kind of work to do than make those gadgets, aint there. Not that any he American wants to do, said Willie, believe me, we want to work making gadgets, and that's what we'll all do, we will stand in line till we get a job to make gadgets, and somebody else will stand in line till he gets a job to sell them on the installment plan. And then, said Jo, we use up all our raw material which is what makes us so rich. Sure we will, said Willie, and then we'll all be dead, and why worry. I do worry, said Brewsie, Sure you worry, said Willie, that's why we love you and that's why we listen to you, we like you to worry, go ahead and worry.

Yes, said Brewsie, yes let me explain, I understand everything. Sure you do, said Willie. This, said Brewsie, is what I understand, and it's terribly important, even if you dont listen, well you got to listen, listen. It's not about jobs but yes it is about jobs, you see industrialism, you know making a lot of things turning them out just like that by the million in no time, England began it, early in the nineteenth century. If I'd known those Limies invented it, I never would go home to get a job, I'd stay right here, said Willie. Well they did, said Brewsie, they invented it and they made machines and they turned out well not like we do but a hell of a lot of goods but they had all their colonies to dump them on and their possessions, you know about how the sun never set on them, it never shines on them that's all I know, said Jo. Well anyway they had lots of coal and iron ore and tin right there on that island and they just made and made, and everybody gave up every kind of way of living excepting jobs in factories and mines, even little children, and they made all their colonies and empire buy them and it was swell just like us and they got richer and richer. Well we horned in after our Civil War, we went industrial and we had more everything than they had and we got richer and they got poorer and their markets that is the people in their empire slowed down in buying and they used up their raw material, and then they tried to take new places to sell to, like Egypt which they took from the French and Africa from the Dutch. The lousy Limies, said Willie. You just wait, said Brewsie, and there we were getting richer and richer and why because we had our outside market right at home that is we had emigration, thousands and millions coming in every year into our country, and as soon as they made some money. The lousy foreigners, said Willie. Well anyway they made America rich I tell you that Willie, and they bought and they became us, yes U.S. us, and the more they came the more they made and like England we kept on using up our raw material and it was fine. Well Germany and Japan they said they'd get industrial too, but they had no raw material but they said they'd buy up stocks of raw material and they'd manufacture and they'd get countries that had raw material and own them, Germany would own Russia and Japan China. Well well, said Jo, that's just what they did do, I mean that's just what they didnt do. Yes, said Brewsie, but it wasnt so easy to stop them. And it's all because everybody just greedy wants to manufacture more than anybody can buy, well then you know what happened after the last war we cut off immigration, we hoped to sell enough to foreign countries, foreign countries didnt want to buy and we had the depression. My God yes, said Jo, we did have the depression. Yes and then we had to fight, and yes we won but we used up a hell of a lot of raw material and now we got to make a club to make those foreign countries buy from us, and we all got to go home to make some more of those things that use up the raw material and that nobody but our own little population wants to buy. Oh dear, said Brewsie.

Oh dear, said a woman's voice behind him, it does just sound too awful. Yes, said another woman, my father used to say it would happen, I remember now, he was an Englishman and he did used to say it would happen. A Limey, muttered Willie. Well he did say it would happen, and he said when they cut off immigration he said to me little girl you'll see right here in this big rich prosperous country you'll see a real depression, not just busted booms but a real big depression. But Brewsie, said Jo, what you mean, what can any of us do but go home get a job if we can, make the gadgets you say nobody has the money to buy, and buy them ourselves on the installment plan and borrow money from Friendly Finance to sort of worry along, what can we do, what you want us to do want us to starve, you cant starve with that all that land that has fallen out of cultivation. Sure not, said Richard, didnt I tell you about my two hundred acres. Yes, said Jo you're sitting pretty, but we cant all be farmers, what the hell can we do. That's what the English are saying, said one of the women. Oh sister forget the Limies. But, said she, how can I forget them when we are doing just like them. I

know, said Brewsie. I know, said Richard. Well I
dont know I'm going to believe it even if it is true,
said Willie. If it is true, said Jo, you got to believe
it. I dont see why I got to believe a thing only because it's true, said Willie. Well, said Jo, what you
going to believe. Perhaps I wont believe anything,
said Willie, you can do that, I dont say I will do it,
but I say you can do it. He certainly is right, said
Richard Paul you certainly can get along fine and
not believe it even if it is true. Anyway what if it is
true it dont prove anything. I aint going to get a
job that's all I know, I'd rather be a tramp. Will
you, said one of the girls, will you be a tramp. No
I wont have to, a fellow like me always lives easy
some way. Yes you do, said Jo. Listen, said one of
the girls, I heard some men talking. Frogs, said
Willie, you didnt believe them. No they werent
frogs they, well they did say and I know that my
father would have thought so too. It's enough, said
Willie, that we got to fight the rich men and the
poor men too, but we got to stop somewhere sister,
we cant take on your father, sure anybody has to
have a father, that's all right but anybody can forget about a father especially in a war, especially.
Well, said the nurse, it is especially in a war you
better find out something, that is what those guys
in the Intelligence say and do they.

Jo: Let her talk.

Willie: Any sister has the right to talk about her father, any sister.

It isnt about my father it was about what some men said, they said, those men said, why do the Americans make such a fuss, and everybody should be grateful to them, what's the matter with them said these men dont they know they didnt come over to Europe to fight until they were attacked at Pearl Harbor and then they came over to protect the rear of their country, and then well they crossed the channel all right but they were fighting a pretty broken German army which had all its best troops killed in Russia, and they thought France fine when they had the French resistance to help them but when they got to Germany with no guerrillas to help them, it did not go so good, and then the Germans almost broke through with a used-up army. Janet, said one of the women in a shocked voice, Janet did you sit there and listen to those men say things like that about your country. It was their country too, it was, they were Americans, and Janet you mean to say you sat there and listened to Americans talk like that about America about the American army. I didnt sit Jenny I stood and anyway it is true. It isnt true Janet it is not true, nothing is true that makes the American army sound like that, I am going home, and you will find out how wrong you were. Dont forget sister, said Jo, she had a father. And I, said Willie, met two soldiers just yesterday who never have and never can worry, and why cant they and why dont they worry, well because they're too young, they are so young they just smile, dont you worry, sister even if your name is Jenny dont you worry there are a lot of them too young to worry, they just smile.

CHAPTER

Seven

DOES IT MAKE one mad or doesnt it make one mad, said Willie. What you mean, asked Jo. Well, said Willie, I saw a Negro soldier sitting on a bench just looking out into the street, and next to him were three white women, not young, not paying any attention nor he wasnt paying any attention to them and I didnt know whether it made me mad or didnt make me mad. Well, said Jo, I kind of notice they all think they still care and they think it makes 'em mad but really it doesn't make 'em mad not even when they see a white woman walking with one of them, the boys like to think it makes 'em mad but it doesnt really make 'em mad not really it doesnt. No, said Willie, I guess it just really doesnt, perhaps because they've griped so much they kind have lost the trick of getting mad or perhaps they just dont care, not the Southern fellows and not anybody really very much. Well I know, said Jo,

41

when I was in school down in Paris the only Red Cross place where you could get coffee and doughnuts anywhere near was a colored one and so we just all went in there, and just at first we never went in alone, we just always were two or three together and then just anyhow kind of soon we went in alone or together just as it happened and we sat down anywhere and we ate coffee and doughnuts and we just didnt think a thing about it not at any time, no I dont know whether we just lost the way of getting mad. There arent any fellows just mad much anyway, sometimes when they see some Negroes sitting just like that in a café, they look at them as if they feel they ought to get mad about it, but nobody notices and they just dont kind of remember to keep on being mad about it. Yeah, said Ed, lots of the boys they say wait till we get home we'll show these Negro soldiers and officers where they belong, and they say it just to kind of hearten themselves up about being at home but they just cant feel mad about it, they just cant, I never have seen any that really can. I saw two soldiers once, they said, what part of town do the Negroes go to because we dont want to go anywhere near that. Yes sure you dont I said, but how do you know there is that part of town. Well there always is these two soldiers said and we see enough of Negroes, we

42

work with them over supplies. Well and dont you get along, no we dont, said the two soldiers and we dont come from the South, we come from the way North. All right, I said, and they said all right, and that was that. Say, said Richard, I heard a Negro man say a funny thing, somebody did say to him somebody said he had a dog there who only talked English. Only talk English, does he, said the Negro man, well then I guess I certainly do not ever want to interrupt him. I often wonder, said Brewsie, whether home was ever like this. Well you can be sure it never is like this, said Willie. Yes I know, said Brewsie, but I mean when we get home will we get mad and all excited up about something that really doesnt amount to anything to us just like we did before there was this war. I do wonder, said Brewsie. You always are wondering, said Willie. I met two soldiers and they said you know what happened to one of us the other night. He drew a pistol on a German girl he had because he didnt trust her. And what had she done, I said. She hadnt done a thing except what she was there to do, but he heard a noise just a little noise and so he drew a pistol on her. And what did she do. She was scared, that's what she did. Well, said Ed, anyway you look at it girls, well we have to have them, an American soldier has to have wine women and song, he just is made that way. Oh is he, said Willie, you just listen to Brewsie. Well what of it, it's true anyway. Not so true, said Brewsie, not so true, kind of true but not so true. Pin-up girls, not so true, said Brewsie, wait till you get home and have to treat girls in an ordinary way, not so much wine women and song. You think you're soldiers and you make yourselves up like soldiers and soldiers have to have wine women and song, and so all American soldiers just are so sure they have to have wine women and song, American soldiers think life is a movie and they got to dream the parts in their feelings. Here comes some more sisters, said Willie. I wish we wasnt so popular, said Willie.

For all that, said Jo, you know what I was doing, I was coming along and I stopped before a door and there was a crack in a door and when I looked through and there she was, a whore. Did you go in, asked Willie. No I didnt go in, said Jo, and you wouldnt have gone in either, said Jo. Well, said Willie, I want to know. I, said Ed, I was coming along and there was a girl and she said to me you stand over across the street in front of that little door and when I tell you you commence and sing a song. And did you, said Willie. Well, said Ed, yes I did go across the street and I stood in front of the door and then she said she was there back across the street and she said sing and I began to sing. What did you sing, said Willie. Oh just a song and when I got started singing that song she said, stop, and I stopped. How come, said Jo, that you understood her, said Jo. Well I did understand her, said Ed. And then what happened, said Willie. Well, said Ed, when I got back across the street she was gone. Where did she go to, said Willie. I dont know where she went to all I knew was that she was gone. And what did you do then, said Willie. I went back across the street and finished the song. I dont guess you did, said Willie. The nurses were there by that time. We would like, said the nurses, if you would tell us about what you were talking about the last time. You never want him to say twice what he said once, said Willie. No of course, said the nurse, no of course not but just the same I wish that he would talk and if only he would I am sure a great many, a very great many would like to listen. He's modest, said Willie, you are modest Brewsie, that's what you are, said Willie, but just the same you tell them Brewsie, everybody wants to hear you tell it, begin now. Yes do begin now, said the nurses. Well all the same, said Brewsie, I will begin now. I worry, said Brewsie, we all worry, said Brewsie, and said Jo, we got plenty to worry us. Not now, said Brewsie, not now, now when we are soldiers and fed and clothed and taken sightseeing. No, said Brewsie, not now, we only think we are worrying now, but when we get home and bills, and pay your way, and we are lazy, that's what we are, lazy. Not so lazy, said Ed, not so lazy. No, said a nurse and her name was Pauline, you know what I often think, I often think, that we dont really hate everybody the way everybody says they do, no we really dont, but we are just kind of scared and lost, and we want to go home. Being a soldier I often think, said Pauline, is all right when there is fighting, fighting knocks the scare out of you, the scare of being alone. You never are alone when you are fighting. I know that even when there is only one in a fox hole, you are not really alone because there is danger there but when the danger is all over like it is now and you are away from home where everybody is just like you and you have that comfort, when they are all just like you, like they are at home, when you are home too, but when you are away from home and there is no more danger and excitement of danger then the boys really feel all alone and they have to be really tough to give them courage and they have to hate everybody to give themselves courage. They certainly have to sister, said Willie. They certainly have to and they do, said Jo. They certainly do hate everybody they certainly do, said Ed, and they are going to go on hating them until they get home and then, said Donald Paul. Then, said Ed, then I dont know. Well Brewsie, now sister has talked, you talk and tell us how to save ourselves from death and measles, said Willie. Death aint so bad, said Jo, but measles, did any of you ever have measles, said Jo. You shut up tight Jo, everybody has had measles, let Brewsie begin. Well I am going to begin, said Brewsie, because I have a lot to say and I am going to say it all and it is going to take me a lot of time. We'll wait, said the nurses. Let's begin about the Civil War, said Brewsie, the great war of the Civil War, said Brewsie, well it was a mistake. And, said Jim at that, that's no news, it certainly was one hell of a mistake, I come from Georgia, mistake is the word. Well you missed your steaks all right, said Willie. Yes we did, said Jim and for a mighty long time but we're beginning to eat 'em up now. I wonder, said Jo, I did my training way down South, yes I did. Most as foreign as foreigners, said Willie, only you got to be polite, you cant call 'em lousy foreigners because that way they arent foreigners, they are lousy and they are foreigners but they are not lousy foreigners, not not, you get me. My aunt, said Donald Paul, I have an aunt somewhere down there and she told me her mother a sweet old lady said to her about the

Yankees who were down there training, remember my daughter we must be patient with them because we must always remember that they are after all our allies, even if they are Yanks they are our allies. Remember that daughter. Yes, said Brewsie, I keep telling you we have to go back to that Civil War, that long Civil War, that American Civil War and it was a mistake, the South should never have fought, she should have let her slaves be bought off, slavery is wrong whatever you say you cant take any man and take away his wife and children if he dont want them to go and they dont want to go, and sell 'em to somebody else, it's not right. Well, said Jim, nobody in the South talks about that any more. No but all I say the South shouldnt have fought. But, said Donald Paul how about state's rights, that's what they fought for. Well that's just it, said Brewsie, they didnt because if they wanted state's rights the way to have done was to let their slaves be compensated for, and they would then have been so strong politically they would have beaten out on state's rights. I tell you, said Brewsie, the Civil War it was a mistake, and we are all suffering for it. How come, said George, why you suffering. Because, said Brewsie, the South it would have acted as a brake on the North. A kind of dead weight you mean, said Willie. Not necessarily

48

dead, said Jim. No, said Brewsie, not necessarily dead but a counterweight, keeping us from going ahead so fast. Oh dear, sighed the nurse Pauline, oh dear, we have to find a way so they say not to go down to poverty after eighty paltry years of wealth like England did with industrialism. You got a father too who was a Limie, said Willie. I have not my father was good American even if he did believe in Bryan. Who's Bryan, said Willie, I had a father who believed in Single Tax, his name not my father's but Single Tax's name was Henry George, all right Brewsie, you go on when we were yes we were fighting so no colored man would ever again have to say yes ma'am, thank you ma'am. Well that's something I do get kind of tired of that word ma'am. I've heard a lot of Southerners say it an awful lot of times. Ma'am, all right we fought that Civil War so that would not happen any more. Well yes, said Brewsie. Now, said Brewsie, I want you all to listen to me. You listen to me, said Donald Paul, I got something real to say, the trouble with us all, all Americans, they think they are up to date but they are just old-fashioned. Just old-fashioned, said Pauline, old-fashioned. My father never said that, and he said almost anything. Well, said Donald Paul, then I move on, not that I am not old-fashioned too like you all, it makes me cry and wish my name was Christopher when I realize how old-fashioned we all are. Old-fashioned, said Donald Paul, old-fashioned, what we think about war what we think about Germans, we think about 'em just like the last lot did twenty-five years ago, yes we do. We like 'em the Heinies, because they have electric lights and fixings, if there is anything old-fashioned it's that, just old-fashioned. They tell me that the gypsies in Spain had electric lights fifty years ago, why make such a much of it, no we're old-fashioned. We think war is wine, women and song, and heroes, we're just old-fashioned, we believe in industrialism, which makes us poor, we are just bloody old-fashioned, old-fashioned, old-fashioned, old-fashioned. Dont you, said Willie, dont you get so excited, yeah, old-fashioned, yes said Donald Paul just as old-fashioned as a pin-up girl, what's the matter with a pin-up girl. Nothing the matter with a pin-up girl, if only you know it's old-fashioned. Do you know, said Pauline with great solemnity, you know that Stein woman who says things. Yeah we all know, said Willie. Well she said America that is the United States of America is the oldest country in the world because she went into the twentieth century in eighteen ninety, when all the others were way behind and so now the United States of America instead of being young and vigorous is old like a man of fifty, still a chippy chaser cause he feels so young, but conservative, just like we are. Oh my oh my, said Pauline, I am glad my father believed in Bryan. Well, said Janet, do you think then it is kind of right and a mighty good thing they are striking over home and not working, kind of tough on everybody not earning anything but since all the countries want us to work and use up our raw material just to give them things. It's perhaps all right that they are striking. See how they like it those countries that want us to give them everything, see how they like doing without. Fine sister fine, your father certainly did for sure believe in something, it certainly does seem so. But, said Jane, aint it a little bit cutting off your nose to spite your face. Well why do you mind that sister, said Willie, why you so old-fashioned.

It was coming on winter, it always is coming on winter when summer is over and it was coming on winter and even if everybody does eat his supper or dinner at five o'clock, it comes on dark when it comes on winter. Did you ever, said Christopher, did you ever hear anything so funny. They just kicked out a lot of Heinies out of their houses, told 'em they had to quit in eight hours because they needed just all those houses. And what do you think

STRAHORN LIBRARY
COLLEGE OF IDAHO

those Heinies did, instead of packing up and finding some place to roost, they just started in cleaning the house from top to bottom to leave it all nice and clean for us soldiers. Did they really, said Pauline. They really did and do, said Ed. That does make them old-fashioned, said Jim, my God yes. I hope, said Brewsie, that they are not so old-fashioned that they are new-fashioned, that'll never happen to them. Or to us, said Donald Paul. Oh shut up everybody, said Willie, I wish Brock was here, I never did wish for that guy before but he would say something so long-winded it would be funny and my God you need something funny, nothing's funny, nothing, not even the American soldier or a Heine, no nothing's funny nothing, not even the comics no nothing nothing, no nothing nothing is funny.

Eight

Do you know, said Ed, Brewsie is right he just is, those wine women and song guys, Brewsie's right they dont care about girls not really. It was like this. One of those actor girls and a mighty fine-looking Jane she is, well she went out to dinner with two of us and we asked her to dress up in civvies, so we could feel like we were home, there were two of them and they did, and after dinner it was a nice night and we walked on home, it was awful, lots of G.I.s were drunk, some not so drunk they came up to us and they used the most God-awful language about just anything and there were crowds everywhere and not one single one noticed that there was a mighty good-looking real American girl with us, good as any pin-up they ever pinned up, but because she did not wear a label saying pin-up not one of those fellows not one of them ever noticed that she was there, they thought if they thought, a fellow has picked up a frog, they didnt even notice not any of them that if it was a frog girl it was a mighty good-looking one, no not any of them not one of them noticed, and then you say Brewsie aint right. It's all make believe to give 'em courage and make 'em real tough, they dont really notice a thing not a thing when it is a girl.

How, said Willie, can they notice when the part of them that aint drunk is worrying about jobs. How I hate that word job, said Brewsie. You're right, said Willie, you're right to hate that word, hate it good and plenty, but you can afford to hate it Brewsie, fellows like you dont need a job you just live, everybody's got to see to it you live and live you do but fellows like us, well we got to have jobs, what you want us to do, nobody's going to feed us, you just watch them not feed us dont we know, no we got to have jobs, talk all you like and talk is good I like talk I like to listen to you Brewsie, but when we get home and dont wear this brown any more we got to have a job, job, job. Yes job. I know, said Brewsie, I know, I know Willie. Yes I know, you got to have a job, and it's all right but it's not all right, see here let me tell you about jobs. Some have to have jobs, some have got to be employed and be employees, but not so many

54

Willie. Listen to me not so many, when everybody is employed. God, said Willie, if they only just could not be employed. I aint forgot that depression, no not yet. Yes but Willie, said Brewsie, that's what I want to say, industrialism which produces more than anybody can buy and makes employees out of free men makes 'em stop thinking, stop feeling, makes 'em all feel alike. I tell you Willie it's wrong. All right, said Willie, it's wrong. I'll say it's wrong, I aint so sure I dont think it's wrong, and there is that old man Kaiser, making poor California come all over industrial. I liked my California, said Willie, yes I did like my California. Yes I know you liked your California, said Brewsie, yes I know. But listen Willie now we are alone let's go all over this and get it straight. Will you let me. You know, said Willie, I never did think I could ever be homesick for that man Brock but I am, how it would kind of cheer me up just to hear his foolishness about how his father and his mother or is it his mother grew their flowers, grew them on their own graves perhaps but it would be a kind of a comfort to hear him, yes and how they moved from one house to another. Well go on Brewsie, go on straighten things out. I'm sure straight is something that looks funny, but go on, let's straighten it out. Well, said Brewsie, it's about this industrialism. You know, said Willie, what you make industrialism sound like, you make it sound like chewing gum. You chew and chew but it dont feed you, it's got a kind of a taste but that is all there is to it no substance. Have I got it right, kind of. Industrialism is like chewing gum. Well go on Brewsie I am here to hear.

Let's go all over it carefully from the beginning, said Brewsie.

Do you know, said Jo, a funny thing happened to me, I just took me a room in a hotel you know one of those little hotels in a little street and I was standing in the doorway and a Negro soldier came along and he said hello to me and I said hello to him and at the end of that little street there came down another street two M.P.s and nothing happened, said Jo.

Well listen, said Brewsie, we got to talk this over earnestly, we got to use all our common sense and see what there is to do. Well if there is anything to do can we do it, said Jo. No we cant do it, said Willie. The thing to do, said Brewsie is to use all our common sense. Well I got plenty of that, said Willie, go ahead Brewsie.

If, said Brewsie, industrialism is wrong not because of this or not because of that but because in a very little while it makes the country going all industrial poor, well then it aint common sense to go on being industrial. That's right, said Jo. Yeah that's common sense, said Willie. Well listen, said Brewsie, it's so, let's go over it again, to see how the countries go poor which are industrial and how that is inevitable. Now look at France she never went industrial and she is rich. Now is she now, said Willie, if she is, then I guess I just as leave be poor even if I have to be industrial. The frogs. Yes but you see France dont get poor because she makes luxuries, and you cant be industrial and make luxuries because once industry makes luxuries it aint a luxury any more. Yeah, said Willie, I know that's it just like that, dont we all spend all we got right here in this France, dont we, and we dont spend it nowhere else. Yes it's good sense that, but cause we spend does that make her rich. Yeah course it does, said Jo, because what she sells dont cost her hardly anything to make, while when it's industrial so many got to be paid and so much raw material it makes you poor. It dont, said Willie, seem to make sense. I know it's all true but all the same just the same it does not seem to make sense. Just the same, said Brewsie, it does make sense, now listen. Here come the sisters, you might as well wait till they get here. Yes, said Pauline, here we are, now tell us. Yes, said Jane, tell us tell us tell us why, no I dont mean to be funny. Perhaps you're not funny said Jimmie. Well anyway we all understand when you say, said Janet, that we Americans, that is to say that we are the last of the countries that went industrial in the nineteenth century who have not yet gone poor, but you say we will. I wonder, said Jo, why now everybody that is all of us call America the States, in the old days that is before now, Americans always call it America or the United States, it was only foreigners who called it the States, and now just as natural as anything we each one and every one of us calls it the States just like some foreigners like the Limies used to. I wonder, said Pauline, I wonder does that really mean anything does that mean the beginning that we are beginning to feel poor, call it the States instead of America, do you think, said Pauline, do you think it does really mean anything. Everything means something, said Donald Paul, dont you know that, havent you heard, that's what's called psychoanalysis, dont you know that, that says anything always means something. And dont you know, said Jimmie, that's true in science too, anything means something. Perhaps, said Donald Paul, something means anything, perhaps it's more like that. Ah you all talk too much, said Willie, give Brewsie a chance. Brewsie is sort of timid, give Brewsie a chance. What we all here for, we are all here to listen to Brewsie, give Brewsie a chance, you go ahead Brewsie. Now before you talk any more I want to ask something, said Jane, is there going to be any answer because if there isnt going to be any answer, I think I'll go back. Is there going to be any answer. Is there going to be any answer Brewsie, the sister wants to know, she's very polite but she certainly does want to know. Yes, said Brewsie, I do think there is an answer. I am kind of coming to it, of course it has to be that we have to take care of ourselves. Well, said Jimmie, there is one thing not anybody has any doubt about whatever he thinks that if we dont take care of ourselves, no industrialist boss, any name you like to put to them not any one of them is going out of his way to take care of us, take care of ourselves is right, take care, take care, all right we'll take care but how, striking is no good if anybody is poor, wanting more work is no good, if working more work uses up our raw material and makes us all poor, how in hell you going to answer the sister Brewsie, and answer me too Brewsie, and yourself too, how you going to answer us all or any of us just how can you, if you are right and my God it does kind of seem so, the more we work the poorer our country gets and the more depressions we have. What's the answer Brewsie, dont keep us on the anxious seat, if you got an answer my God dont keep it to yourself, give it to us. I say Brewsie give it to us. Well, said Brewsie, yes but do you mind all of you if I begin all over again from the beginning. I guess the boys are right, said Pauline, we cant help ourselves if we do mind, and we do mind, we'd like the answer now yes we would but all right, go on begin begin anywhere but goodness gracious do begin. Be quiet sister, said Willie, you make him kind of nervous and if he gets too nervous everything kind of stops and if everything stops he'll never get going again and then where will we be, what will happen, we'll just be poor, poor, poor white trash. Perhaps, said Donald Paul it will be the niggers who get rich, I suppose even in a poor country somebody has just got to be rich. Not always, said Willie, look at the Limies. My father, said Janet. Yeah your father, said Willie. But let Brewsie talk, see he is opening his mouth, not good and wide yet, but let him tell us how to be useful but poor. No, said Brewsie, how to be hopeful though poor. At that, said Jo, at that, hope is something. But, said Jane, if we had not been industrial the way we were how we would have won this war. Did we win it, said Willie. Yes, said Jane, we did, we did win this war. Well then, said Donald Paul, with that behind us we can settle down to be poor but honest. Not so much on the honest, said Pauline, ever hear about stealing. Stealing what, said Jo. Go anywhere in the occupied country and what does everybody do. They steal. Sure they do, said Willie, and then they gamble it away and they go home poor but honest. Poor it is, said Jo. I know. Good God, said Jimmie, everybody shut up. Go ahead Brewsie, how about what the sister says, how about that winning the war, how about it, what's the answer Brewsie, what's the answer.

CHAPTER

Nine

LISTEN WILLIE, said Brewsie, you kind of think I
go over it all too much, you're like anybody with a
story, you want the middle to go faster but that's it
Willie, that's it, it is going too fast, got to slow
it down, got, sure then you want the end, but Willie
there isn't any end, you got to go slower, sure there
is an answer. I kind of feel the answer, sometimes I
know I know the answer, but wait Willie, wait till
I tell you all about it all over, perhaps if I tell you
all about it all over you'll come to the answer too,
not an answer but a way to go on, wait Willie while
I tell you all about it from the beginning. I got
nothing to do but wait, said Willie, not just right
here, not anything to do but wait, but when we get
back and then hustle. Yes but Willie, that is what
you dont see it is not hustle you got to slow down,
Willie, that is what has to happen, it has to slow
down, when you get back you have to pioneer, and

pioneering is slow work. Pioneer what, said Willie. Pioneer, said Brewsie, listen to me Willie, I am so earnest, listen to me Willie. I said Henry, before I came into the army I taught the seven year olders in public schools. Where, said Jo. In western New York state. Was that interesting, said Jo. Well yes it was sometimes it was almost exciting. And, said Jo, are you going back to it. Well no, said Henry, not if I can get a job over here. What, said Willie, you want to stay in this lousy Europe. Well yes in a way, said Henry, you see my mind's confused, and so I want to stay. Willie, muttering mind mind, confused, get a mind, get it confused, I suppose, said Willie, you have been listening to Brewsie. No I havent, said Henry. Who's Brewsie. Who's Brewsie, said Willie, that's Brewsie, well how did you get your mind confused if you didnt listen to Brewsie. Well I guess, said Henry, I got my mind confused because I just cant see any way not to have my mind confused that's all, see here Willie, you see it's about that employee mentality we're all getting to have, we're just a lot of employees, obeying a boss, with no mind of our own and if it goes on where is America, I say if it goes on, where is America, no sir, said Henry, no sir, I want to pioneer. Ah, said Willie, you been listening to Brewsie. I have not been listening to Brewsie. I dont know Brewsie,

63

never saw him, less heard him, you listen to me Willie. You see I been in England, and that country is poor poor, and it's poor because it went industrial and the people lost their pep they went employee-minded and they manufactured more than they could sell and they speeded it up, and they went bust and I am kind of scared about going home. You know what Churchill said he did not want to preside over the downfall of the British empire. Well I dont want to see us get more employee-minded, employed by the big factory owners, employed by the strikers, employed by the government, employed by the labor unions. Well, said Willie, who the hell do you want should employ you who the hell do you want should give you a job. I dont want a job, said Henry. I want to pioneer. Oh hell, said Willie, you make me tired, you been listening to Brewsie, and anyway you want to get a job over here. How that, you a pioneer. Well that's different, said Henry. How different, said Willie. Well it is different, said Henry, because anyway there are a few of us and so we can forget we are just employed, anyway that's something, said Henry. You get the hell out of here you been listening to Brewsie and at that, Brewsie he would never be so silly as thinking of getting a job over here was pioneering. Come over here Brewsie,

64

explain to this guy what pioneering is. I dont know yet, said Brewsie, I am just thinking. Well let's all think, said Henry. No, said Willie, you let Brewsie do the thinking, that's the way we are in this outfit, we let Brewsie do the thinking. Willie, said Brewsie, Yes, said Henry, that just shows how employee you are Willie. Oh get the hell out of here, said Willie. Yeah it's funny, said Jimmie, the only real pioneering there is in America these days is done by Negroes. They're pioneering, they find new places, new homes, new lives, new ways and they more and more own something, funny, said Jimmie, kind of queer and funny. I dont like it, said Jo. No, said Jimmie. No I dont like it, said Jo, it makes me kind of nervous. Does it, said Jimmie, well it doesnt make me nervous, I guess when you come from the South anything like that dont make you kind of nervous. I come from Georgia. Yes I know, said Jo.

Here we are, said Pauline. So you are sister, said Willie. And what are you talking about. We are talking about that, said Willie, what do you think we're talking about women and chickens and yellow butterflies and potatoes, no we just aint talking about them we're talking about that, of course I am not talking I only listen and it never listens good. Yes, said Pauline, but I do want to know.

65

You'll know, said Willie, any moment of the day or night they talk and they always talk about it. About what, said Pauline. About it, about what it is, about how about it, about what is it about, about, what are you going to do about it, about, how about it, you just wait sister you just wait, not that you really have to wait, we got a new guy who talks, his name, what is that guy's name Jo, oh yes his name is, there I lost it again, it dont make no difference all I know is his name is not Brewsie. You better listen to Brewsie, I tell you you better listen to Brewsie. My uncle, said Pauline. Did he believe in Bryan too, said Jo. No, said Pauline, he did not, he was one of the directors of the legion in our town, and he often told me what trouble he had with the last returned soldiers. When they came back to work on their jobs, their bosses complained, they were no good, they were dreamy. Dreamy, said Jane, is a nice way to put it, they must have been polite bosses. I should say that all soldiers and all ex-soldiers come home lazy, that's what I should say, said Jane. Jane, said Janet, be polite, remember you are talking to soldiers and future ex-soldiers. Well it's so all right, said Janet, Sister, said Jo, if you say it it's so but the worst of it is, said Jo, it's so even if you dont say so. I know, said Pauline, my uncle always said that was not all.

He said during the depression he tried to help all the legionnaires and he had ground plowed up so that they could grow food, and they gave them seeds and fertilizer and tools and everything and they mostly said, like the electrician, I am not going to be a farmer, I am an electrician and I'll stay electrician until an electrician job comes my way. I know, said Janet, I know that's the way they are in our town. Well some of them used to go home to work in the gardens and so they started a cinema just where they all took the cars and had a special big attraction just when they might be going home to work in their gardens and so they went to the cinema instead of going home to work in their gardens. That's what my father says. Your father is a Limie isnt he sister. He certainly is one, said Janet and proud to be one. Poor and proud that's what Brewsie would say. Well it's better to be poor and proud than just poor as your Brewsie says you Yankees will be if you dont watch out. Here fellows, said Willie, here we got another one talking, it's catching, you better look out Brewsie, soon there wont be a thing you can tell them. Not at all, said Brewsie, not at all I always keep ahead. Now listen everybody listen. I want to tell you everything all over again and you'll see what I mean. Brewsie, said Willie, if you dont watch out you'll be as tedious as Brock, and that's something. Listen, said Brewsie. I been thinking. Well anyway Brewsie Brock never did begin that way. Go ahead Brewsie we're listening. I wonder, said Jane, could you explain just what President Roosevelt meant when he said that there had to be sixty million jobs, just what did he mean to do, of course we want to know because that would mean women too, just what did he mean to do, can you tell just what did he mean to do. Roosevelt, said Donald Paul, was a benevolent despot and I hate all despots, and benevolent ones are worse than the others because nobody wants to hurt their feelings by telling them so. Yes, said Jane, I know but all the same he just must have meant something. What, said Jo. My father always said so, what is the difference between the New Deal and Communism. Nothing much, said Brewsie, that's why I have to begin all over again because neither of them could be without industrialism, any more than trade unions and capitalists, now that's just it, everything is all right if you dont take too much of it. Like drink and venereal disease, said Willie. Yes that's just it, said Jo, but you see the way I understand it industrialism is not like drink, you can take a little of that the other, well they dig it deep they dig it for one another, and you just cant help falling in and once

68

you're in you cant get out, that's it Brewsie. Not exactly, said Brewsie, not exactly. Well what is it then, said Pauline, what is it, we've got to know. Well not today sister, said Willie, you didnt really got to know today, we got to get home and get a job first and it dont really make all that difference knowing about it today. But it does it does, said Pauline, I have a kind of a feeling and we all have I know we all have if he dont begin to make it begin to come clear today it will never be any better, and he is right, our own dear beautiful strong rich country will go down like England did. Not on your life, said Willie, not on your life. Yeah, said Pauline, that's easy, be the strong white man, who never can be brought down, that's all right if you had never left home, but you have left home, you're scared, you're thinking about every- thing and way back deep down you're scared, scared. I know I am scared too, here I am scared, said Willie, sure you're scared, said Pauline, and he's got to tell us what to do. But, said Brewsie, you got me scared, how can I tell you what to do, I can tell you what's wrong, I can kind of tell you what's going to happen, and it will, said Jane, yes it will. All right, said Willie, it will. I know, said Brewsie, logic is logic, facts are facts I know I am right but how to get going away from what everybody has gotten the habit of thinking is the only way to do, kind of swinging a big truck around, said Jo, and making it come back around a corner. No, said Brewsie, not that, but to find the way that looks the same and is different or find the way that looks different and is the same. Oh dear, said Pauline, we got to hurry up and find out because we're all to be home for Christmas. Does anybody know how old Christmas is, said Willie. Of course, said Pauline, of course read your Bible and you'd know it too. Well, said Brewsie, I begin to know one thing, if industrialism makes a country poor and makes the people of that country poor because they all have employee minds, that is job minds, we got to get on top of industrialism and not have it on top of us. How come, said Jo. Well, said Brewsie, it sounds harder than it is. How do you get on top of anything that is on top of you, first you got to break it off you, said Jo. Oh dear, said Pauline, fighting is so natural.

Ten

YOU GOT TO say it Brewsie, said Willie, you cant just camouflage it, you cant just cover it over, you cant just whisper it, you got to say it and you got to say it out loud. Yes I know Willie, said Brewsie, but you cant say it out loud until it's there to be said. Oh yes you can, said Willie, you'd like to whisper it Brewsie, yes you do just whisper it, but you just got to say it out loud. Yes Willie, said Brewsie, but you got to have it out loud inside you and I tell you I've got it but I havent got it out loud. I've got some of it out loud but not all of it out loud, give me more time Willie, give me time. It aint time, said Willie, it's the way, out loud is the way, got to make a noise, not whisper, said Willie, not whisper. You got to. I know, said Brewsie. I had a little frog kid on my knee, said Jo, and he was very little and I told him to say dog and he learned to say it so quick you'd think he never had talked French, was just learning to talk to say dog. Like anything he said dog, and he didnt forget it, either, he said it again, dog just like that. I guess any kid would, said Jimmie. Well, said Jo, a lady came along and she said is he yours and I said no he's a frog kid but he does say dog, and she said had I one of my own and I said no I been in the army too long and she said how old are you and I said I was twenty-three and she said I did look younger but of course if I had been in the army four years, and I said lady make it five and I said this frog kid says dog, and it did say dog, just like that. I know, said Brewsie. Yes, said Jimmie, you know what they all talking about now at home, they're talking about free trade. My God, said Donald Paul have we come to that. I know, said Jane, my father. And sure he was a Limie and he knew where free trade brings you. Yes, said Jane but he knows more than that, when you know you're going to get poor then you say free trade, when nobody wants to buy them you say free trade, kid yourselves, kid yourselves, the factory owners kid themselves so as to make their workmen believe and the workmen kid themselves with strikes so as to make the owners think they would be working if the men werent striking so they all kid themselves and they kid each other, and does anybody believe. Yeah, said Willie, that's what's so funny about kidding everybody believes, a bigger and better country, a bigger and better industry, a bigger and better war, yeah, sure everybody believes when they kid, they gotta believe, otherwise everybody would stop working. And wouldnt it, said Pauline, wouldnt it just be beautiful if everybody stopped working, and just went out walking, and ate a sundae or an ice-cream soda and went on walking, and then just came home, and had doughnuts and a coke, and then they came in and sing a little and go to bed. How beautiful, said Pauline. Yeah, said Willie, beautiful is the word. I love, said Willie, I love that word beautiful, yes sister I certainly surely do love that word beautiful. Listen, said Ed, listen. I know I just do know. Listen. That sister aint so phony as she sounds, listen. You see like this, when factories work hard and lots of money moves around, then there are chain stores and mail-order houses and little business cant live, cause they cant make enough money to compete, but when the factories they dont work, and everybody just walks around like sister says, why then chain stores and mail-order places go bust, there is too much overhead if there aint a big volume of business, and that's the time for a new start of little business, so that's it boys that's it, if we can stall going home till there is a depression, then we can start our little businesses like we all want to do. How about it everybody, dont that listen good. Say, said Willie, say, it aint Brock come to life again and being different, is it, does anything that guy says make sense or does it. Well I think it does, said Pauline, I certainly do think it does make sense. I wonder, said Willie, Brewsie, where are you Brewsie, did you hear him, where's Brewsie. Brewsie had to go away and think, said Donald Paul. Not Brewsie, said Willie, when Brewsie thinks he stays where he always is, and he always thinks and so he always stays where he is. Brewsie, said Willie, I am here, said Brewsie. Is there, said Willie, any sense to what that guy says. Yes there is, said Brewsie.

CHAPTER

Eleven

I KNOW, said John. What you know, said Jo. I know, said John that I am not just tired of everything not tired of everything, Well that's something to know, said Willie. I know, said John, I am pretty young and I might maybe being so young be just tired of everything, I know what you fellows talk about we all know what Brewsie explains and we all know he's right, that industrialism business makes us all job men with no way of choosing anything, and it'll make the country poor and everybody in it, dont I know, I tell you I know, didnt I see it work, in my family just we we worked out but I know it's right, industrialism makes industrials poor individuals and makes a country poor and I know we're old-fashioned, dont I know all the fellows admire the Heinies, and why, because the Heinies are the only things on this earth that are more old-fashioned than we Americans, and so

75

we kind of suck up to the Heinies to keep 'em in countenance and they suck up to us to kind of keep themselves in countenance, just the most two old-fashioned countries in the world, the least up-to-date in the world, so far behind, they might almost catch up with themselves but they dont and why because they know it but they cant dare hear themselves say it, do I know all this, sure I know all this, I know it's so, and yet and why, well I aint all just tired of everything and sometimes I do almost know why. Dont let anybody stop you telling John, go on, said Willie. Well this is the only thing that kind of comforts me. Come there are lots who know it's all true and wont say, and then there are lots who really know and do say, now I dont believe no I dont that in those countries England, Germany, Japan, no I dont I dont believe a whole young generation knew what was wrong, and were not violent about it, no not at all violent not at all violent, they just knew, that's all they just knew, they just knew it's so. That's the thing that just dont make me just tired of everything, that the big lot of us know all this is so, and they aint a bit violent not a bit, they just know, they just know that this is all so. Yes, said Jo, yes but then what comes next. Does anything come next when you just aint tired of everything, said John. Well, said

Willie, that almost doesnt sound like a question, I'll go get Brewsie. High Brewsie, said Willie, come here Brewsie, somebody got to say something. Where are you Brewsie. He aint there, said Jimmie. Aint he, said Willie. No he aint, said Jimmie.

I dont think, said Ed, that any G.I. would like a Heinie if he were all alone with a Fraulein or a Heinie, he likes Heinies when he's part of a crowd not when the Heinie is although that's all right too but the G.I.s. When there are a plenty of G.I.s, they like the Heinies, now you know if there was only one G.I. alone with some frogs or Mademoiselles he'd like it better than if that same G.I. would be just all alone with Heinies and Frauleins, I kind of sometimes think it would be like that. Well, said John, aint it, that G.I. likes Heinies because like them they like to be a crowd. I heard one G.I. tell a frog that France was too God damn full of Frenchmen, but crowds of Heinies, well do crowds of Heinies make a G.I. feel like a strong man, well it's all funny anyway but I dont care, said John, I just dont care. All I care about is that I just aint just all tired of everything. And that's good thing too, said Willie.

But what we gonna do, said Ed, not about Heinies, Heinies is just dirt, you know, said Peter another thing is funny and that is fluffy food, not chow, you dont mean, said Willie, I see no fluff in chow. Yeah, I do, said Peter. We love sweets like babies, we dont love no lumps of cheese, and tough bread, no we just like to eat soft stuff, soft bread, soft ice-cream, soft chocolate, soft mush, soft potatoes, soft jam, and peanut butter, we dont except at a little meat we dont really chew. Well and if we dont, said Jo. Soft eats make soft men, said Peter. We soft, are we, said Willie. Well aint we, said Peter. Well perhaps we are, said Willie. How soft, said Jo. Too soft, said Ed. Well where is Brewsie, said Willie, where is Brewsie. I'd even like to hear a sister speak up just for a change. Where is that Brewsie. Listen to me, said Brewsie, although really I havent anything really to say. We're listening, said Willie, with a sigh of relief.

Twelve

Do WE, said Brewsie, that is to say do they know just who we are while we wear brown and if they do know just who we are does that give us distinction. Now, said Willie, you're talking funny and when you talk funny you know how old I am. How old are you Willie, said Jo, you know, said Jo, they used to say be your age and I kind of wonder sometimes are we that age, everybody says we're sad, we know we're lonesome, how old do you have to be to be sad, and how young can you be to be lonesome. Yes, said Donald Paul, everybody is talking funny, is it because perhaps isnt that a nice word, redeployed, redeployed. Hell, said Willie, redeployed it is, they make it like that because they wont be responsible if we have a job or not. Dont you know, said John, that Brewsie dont like that word job. He never said, said Jo, that he liked that word redeployed. Funny, said Donald Paul, very funny, and

sometimes nobody knows how funny it is, redeployed. I know, said Jim, I met a man who was
born in Mississippi, he couldnt read and write.
And can he now, said John. He just can and as
good as I can. Well well, said Donald Paul, well
well. Dont you get funny, said Jimmie, if you get
very funny, oh hell, said Willie, let's go home.
What home, Heaven, said John. No not Heaven,
said Willie, just home just redeployed just home.
Sometimes, said Jo, I am scared. Sometimes, said
Willie. Just sometimes, said Jimmie. Why does
anybody want to be scared all the time. Just the
same, said Donald Paul, what are you going to do.
I, said Brewsie, I been thinking. Oh, said Willie,
that's what makes me all here, go on Brewsie,
think. My God Brewsie think, if you dont think
Brewsie. Yeah, said Jo, you always want somebody
to do your thinking for you. Well why not, said
Jimmie, why not, said Jo, why not. Oh of course
why not think, Brewsie, if you can, it's kind got
near redeployment, Brewsie, think Brewsie, think.
My God yes Brewsie think, we're getting older and
older Brewsie, just think. Yeah, said Jimmie, and
after all does it do any good. Yes it does, said John,
it keeps us talking. And does that do any good, said
Jo. Yes it does, said John, it does, we'd go crazy if
Brewsie didnt think, crazy. Well, said John, if you

dont like that word redeployment, if that does make you kind of nervous, how about that word reconversion, how do you like that all you, how do you. That, said Donald Paul, that is only a word, reconversion turns out to be only a word. A third of a word, said Jimmie, it might have made you feel like a bird, but it only turned out to be a third of a word. I know, said Brewsie, I told you so, you remember I told you so, I said remember that those industrialists know as well as I do that there arent any foreign markets and do they want to start, no they dont, so they let them strike and so it aint their fault, the others and everything is as it is. It's lousy, said Willie, yes it is. More lousy than foreigners Willie, said Donald Paul. Almost not yet quite but well no not that not as lousy as foreigners no no not that, never that, foreigners are lousy, everything is lousy but foreigners they are all lousy. It's funny, said John, when I see one of those frogs with one of those large loaves of bread under his arm, I know he is going to have good eats, you cant not not with that bread. Yeah, said Willie, I like that bread, And I like the cafés, said Jo, they are real comfortable, winter and summer they are real comfortable. And, said Jimmie, it's kind of nice when you are riding along in a truck to see all that landscape and no billboard. I kind of like billboards, said Willie, it is one of the things I do kind of like, said Willie. Brewsie, said John, you know I am young, I got no points, I aint been over long and when I get out I kind of think I'll stay over here a while. But Brewsie tell me if I was not so young and had more points and was not going to stay over a while and I was going home what could I do about it, tell me Brewsie, they say you can, tell me Brewsie. Well, said Brewsie, what is it we got that nobody else has got. The atomic bomb, said Jo. Not so got, said Jimmie, they all say not so got. All right then not the atomic bomb, said Jo, tell us Brewsie what we got that nobody else has got. Well, said Brewsie, I think we still have got it, we like to pioneer. How can you pioneer when there aint no wilderness any more. Shut up everybody, said Willie, here come the sisters, seems to me more than ever today but there is that cute one they call Pauline. Well go on anyway, said John, how about how you can pioneer when there aint any wilderness. Aint there any wilderness, said Pauline, you just go home and look around, there's lots of wilderness, around where I live there is all wilderness, north south east and west, and where is it you live sister, said Willie. Oh I just live, said Pauline. All right then, said Jo, you just live. Well can anyone pioneer in that wilderness of yours. Why not, said

82

Pauline. Anybody can say why not, said Willie, but do you mean it sister, can anybody pioneer where you live. Yes they can if they got any guts and dont expect it to to be easy. All right sister, said Willie. Now listen to me, said Janet, I think he is right about that pioneer thing, you got to break down what has been built up, that's pioneering. Why not, said Jo. Yes why not, said Janet, I say if you all are ready to break down what has been built up, well then that is pioneering, here in Europe they broke down what they had built up and now they are all just as busy as anything pioneering and they are kind of happy doing it. Not so happy, said Jimmie, not by their looks. Well anyway, said Janet, they got a lot to do and when you have got a lot to do you are kind of happy and pioneering and we well we havent anything to do not until what we built up has broken down and we can pioneer. But sister, said Willie, you're funny, well I dont want to say all I think because I was brought up to be nice to a lady but what do you want, do you want us to drop our atomic bombs on ourselves, is that what you want, so we can go out and pioneer, is that the idea. Well yes kind of, said Janet. I get you, said Willie. And you get me Willie. Oh, Lord, give me Brock, I never thought I would pray to the good Lord to give me back

Brock but here I am I am praying to the good Lord to give me back Brock. He was awful, but he did sound all right compared to this pioneering idea, he certainly did. But, said John, let's begin again, we've all got kind of funny. Not so funny, said Willie. Well you see, said Brewsie, you do know that we cant keep all together a million or so of us all over our country because in the next war. Oh God, said Willie, the next war, any war we might just as well. Well yes, said Janet, we might just as well think like the Germans, peace is only in between wars and not wars in between peace. Well, said Donald Paul, you see last time everybody thought there was going to be peace and there was war, why not this time everybody think there is going to be war and maybe there will be peace. Maybe, said Willie, But, said John, after all there is our country we got a country, let's think about it we got to think about it, let's think. Well, said Willie, Where is Brewsie. Yes, said Jo, where is Brewsie. Yes, said John, where is Brewsie. Yes, said Janet, where is he. Where is, said Pauline. Where is Brewsie, said Willie. Yes where is he, said Donald Paul.

CHAPTER

Thirteen

WILLIE, said Brewsie, it's serious. Sure it's serious, said Willie, what. Our country, said Brewsie. Sure, it's serious, said Willie. You mean pioneering, she was cute that Pauline about wilderness and pioneering, didnt you think she was cute Brewsie, didnt you. She is cute Brewsie that Pauline. I guess I'll like to see her real often. Yes I would Brewsie, but I guess I will and find out more about her pioneering, she is cute Brewsie. Willie, said Brewsie, it's serious. Yes I know Brewsie, yes I know. All right it's serious but you dont any of you say what to do you all say what's the matter and that everything is the matter but you dont say what to do, thinking is what you do Brewsie, but living is what we all got to do, now what are we going to do, how we going to live. Well, said Brewsie, if I am right they mostly are not going to live. Sure you're right Brewsie but they mostly are going to live, that's it, that's the funny part of it they mostly do go on living, look at the Limies, you're right how poor they are and all and once they were so rich and all but they dont die, they just keep on all of them just going on living, that's the trouble with everything Brewsie, that's the real trouble with everything, somehow everybody just does keep on living, look at everybody over here, by rights they ought all to be all dead, all of them over and over again dead, all of them and they aint Brewsie, they aint at all dead, far from it, from being all dead, they seem from the looks of them to be more of them living than ever were living before, so many more of them, just look at them everywhere is lousy with them and they all ought to be dead but they dont die, that is not more than natural, some more but not really enough more to make it really matter. No Brewsie that's really the trouble with all the thinking that's the real trouble, sure you're right and some get rich and more get poor, and some go ahead and some go behind but all the same they all go on living and so Brewsie, well that is it, sure you're right and if we go on like this well yes we will get poor like the Limies got poor somebody else will get rich like we were rich. Sure Brewsie you're right but in a kind of way we wont die, we'll just all somehow go on living, that's it, Brewsie, that's it, that is what is the matter with thinking, that's it, no matter what does happen everybody somehow goes on living, and there always seem to be lots more of them lots more than anybody needs but they all go on living. Yes, said Donald Paul, that is what William James called the will to live. Yes it is, said Willie, I dont know the guy but that's what it is they just do go on living, you cant kill them off. Dont you make any mistake about that atom bombs or potato bugs or concentration camps or religion or poverty or no jobs or education, it does not make it go any other way, they just do go on living, they dont disappear. The lousy foreigners how many of them God knows how many of them there are, more than ever, I never saw them before but I certainly am fixed to know that there are more of them living than ever, more than ever, that's what I say more of them than ever.

CHAPTER

Fourteen

YES, WILLIE, said Brewsie, yes, but you got to think anyhow. Can you, said Willie, when you are all kind of set that way, can you really make yourself go on when you are all kind of set to get backward. I been reading a book, said John. Well well, said Willie, and here they come that is here they are. Listen sister this guy has been reading a book. Well and if he has so have I, said Janet, I've been reading a book about Susan B. Anthony. And who, said Jo, might that dame be. She is the one, said Janet, that made women vote and have the right to money they earn and to their children, before she came along women were just like Negroes, before they were freed from slavery. You can say what you like but she was pretty wonderful. And if she was, said Willie. Yes I know, said Janet, but the real thing is that she started to do all this because of the depression. My God what depression, said Jo. The depression of eighteen thirty-eight. Now who of all of you ever knew about that not even Brewsie. You know, said Janet, we all think we had the one and only depression, but they began having them in eighteen thirty-eight. Just think of that over a hundred years ago when America first started. Well, said Jimmie, but there was no industrialism then, just wilderness and pioneering, hey Pauline. No, said Janet, and that is what is funny, there was industrialism and it commenced so hard and they had wildcat banking and poof, up went the industries. Nobody had any money to buy just like now. Her father he was well-to-do, he went bust, she had to go to work and she found how little a woman had of her own, a married woman couldnt even have her own money and so she began to make a noise. Now, said Janet, we got to make a noise, a loud noise, a big noise, we got to be heard. Who's we, said Willie, We are all we, said Janet, all of our age all together, we got to make a noise. My name is Lawrence, said Lawrence. Now is it, said Jo, how do you know it is. Well it is, said Lawrence, and I got something to say, she's right, not that it'll do anything, but she's right. The trouble with us is we are being ruled by tired middle-aged people, tired business men, the kind who need pin-ups, you know that kind, only they can afford the originals, not the

89

ones we get, well I tell you, said Lawrence, I tell
you, here in Europe they are ruled by the young
or by the old, and by God they're right, young
ones can make fools of themselves that's all right,
and old ones if they are old enough to be really old
they got the energy of being old, but I tell you and
my name is Lawrence and I tell you old and young
are better than tired middle-aged, nothing is so
dead dead-tired, dead every way as middle-aged,
have we the guts to make a noise while we are still
young before we get middle-aged, tired middle-
aged, no we havent, said Willie, and you know it,
no we havent, said Willie.

CHAPTER

Fifteen

WHAT'S THE MATTER, said Willie. Well it kind of
makes me cry, said Pauline, What makes you cry,
said Willie, well the way you said we hadnt guts
enough to make ourselves heard, it does make me
cry. Yeah but have we, said Willie, Well, said Pauline, it does kind of make me cry.

Sixteen

WILLIE, said Brewsie. Well, said Willie, it is true, said Brewsie, industrialism cant put on a brake itself, nothing quits it down but a catastrophe. How could anything quiet it down, said Willie, do you think anybody knows when they got enough, nobody, said Willie, I tell you Brewsie, nobody ever knows when they got enough. Some do, said John, my mother always did, nothing ever could tempt her to eat a bit more than was enough, she just never did, and she never would run around more than was enough, no Willie, some do have self-control, some do, really Willie, some do. All right, said Willie, some do, but not enough to make any real difference, that's what I mean. Well, said Lawrence, I told you my name was Lawrence and I got something to say, everybody in America they think if perfection is good more perfection is better. I never want to go back, there is no sense to it, none,

I never want to go back. Oh get the hell out of here, said Willie, I know your kind, everything looks good to you except where you belong. All right all right, said Lawrence, all right, I never want to go back. All right, said Willie, dont go back. That's what I am going to do, said Lawrence, I am not going back. All right, said Willie, you're not going back, all right nothing stops anything except hell, well all right, and we got to go back, and what's going to stop anything. But in a kind of a way, said John, nothing has begun. All right, said Willie, and that's right, nothing has begun. Listen, said Brewsie, listen. All right, said Willie, I am so sore, I just could do nothing but listen. All right, said Brewsie, listen, it's true all I said is true all I am saying is true, Willie's right, there arent enough of them got any self-control to stop anything, whether it's drinking or eating or industrialism, or spending. Oh come off, said Jimmie, lots of people got lots of self-control, lots of people have, I even got some of it myself. All right, said Willie, all right then you have and then what. It aint, said Donald Paul, it aint self-control that matters it's what happens that matters, and as nothing is going to happen nothing at all it's that what matters. Now, said, Willie, you're just talking funny. I am not, said Donald Paul, or if I am and perhaps I am then

93

it means something it means a lot, listen. Oh let Brewsie talk. No, said Donald Paul, Brewsie dont know about this, we all go home no re-conversion, no nothing, we kind of dont know what's happening, not a depression, this time just nothing. Well, said Janet, here I am, I heard you. What's nothing. Nothing, said Donald Paul, is when it all stops. Can it, said John. It can, said Donald Paul. Well then, said Jo, what we all going to do we all are there, what we going to do. Well that's it, said Lawrence, some they just kind of will act as if it was just the way it always has been, but most of us we'll know, we'll know that there is just nothing doing nothing. Oh Willie, said Pauline. Now listen to me, said Jimmie, you just listen to me. I got nothing to say but you all just listen to me. All right, said Janet, all right. Well now it's like this, it does kind of scare you that's what he is trying to do, and we, well. We all of us we do scare awful easy, that's what I want to say, we all of us do scare awful easy. Dont everybody scare easy, said John. No I think, said Jimmie, that we kind of scare more easy than lots of others. Because we are spoiled babies, said Janet. I guess that's so, said Jo. Oh dear, said Pauline, I am that scared, well no I am not, I am not scared, I am going home and I am not scared, are you scared

Janet. Well in a way not, said Janet. All right, said Jimmie, we're not scared. All right, said Willie, anyway it's all right. Let's talk, said John. Yes let's, said Jo. I know, said Pauline, you mean it's going to be like a dust-bowl. Yes, said Jimmie, that's it, it's going to be like a dust-bowl. Oh my God, said Jo, I live there. Sure you live there, said Willie, that's what I say anybody can live even in a dust-bowl, that's what I say. Well are we going to live in a dust-bowl, said Pauline. Yes, said Willie, you've said it, we are going to live in a dust-bowl, but live we will, said Willie, why not, said Willie, why not. All right, said Janet, why not. Well, said Pauline, I know why not. Well sister, said Willie, why not. Well, said Pauline, because you all said you were going to pioneer, well and then, and then it wont be a dust-bowl, have you ever read about pioneers, said Lawrence, if you have you'll know a lot about dust-bowls. Oh dear, said Pauline. Oh dear.

Seventeen

You got to, said Willie, you got to Brewsie, you got to hold out a little hope. Yes, said Brewsie, the hope is that our generation is more solid more scared, more articulate than the last ones. What do you mean, said Willie, those G.I.s those guys. Yes I do, said Brewsie, I do mean them. You're crazy, said Willie, they all just think they're the only thing there is, said Willie, they're just nothing, that's what they are, you know what they think, Brewsie, well you just listen. Say, called out Willie, you guys come over here, stop talking about how much you pay for cognac anywhere you are, and how much you got to pay more than anybody else and how much cognac you had yesterday just come over here and tell this man Brewsie what you think lousy foreigners are and what you think Americans are, come over and tell Brewsie, come along over. We Americans, said Sam, we Americans, we ride wide and handsome, that's what we Americans are and everybody admires us. Oh do they, said Donald Paul. Yes they do, why shouldnt they admire us, aint we got everything they want, everything, do they want it, said Donald Paul, sure they want it, said Sam, how could they not want it when they see us have it and we ride so wide and handsome. Wide all right but not so handsome, said Jo. Well, said Paul, if they didnt want what we got would there be any progress. Perhaps there aint any progress, said Donald Paul, perhaps not. There cant not be progress, said Sam, if there isnt any progress how could we sell goods and we gotta sell goods to get a job. Yes, said Donald Paul, that's it. And perhaps said Sam, all these over here they're so poor they live with their chickens and all they're just so poor. Yes all right, said Jimmie, but they do have chickens to live with. Yes, said Sam, but that aint progress. Well I dunno, said Jimmie, I like chickens, I kind of guess there always will be chickens. And if not, said Willie. Well then there might be progress, said Donald Paul, well anyway, said Fred, do you think it's right, that there I was sitting and behaving and I ask for a cognac and then a girl comes in and she has a cognac and then they charge her fifteen and they ask me twenty-five for the same cognac. Not the same, said Jo, hers was hers and yours was yours. And, said Jimmie, anyway you're so rich, you make such a holler that that dollar your dollar is the only money there is, naturally you got to pay more. Sure the dollar is all that, said Fred, but a poor soldier is a poor soldier and he is just poor. Just as poor as a lousy foreigner, said Willie. Well yes kind of, said Jimmie. It's all right, said Fred, it's all right about that dollar, anyway I was sitting there just as peaceable. And, said Donald Paul, you were sitting there with your lonesome dollar. What do you mean, said Fred, I may be a poor soldier but I got more than one dollar. Not that, said Donald Paul, not that, what I mean is that the dollar the United States dollar is a very lonesome dollar, it's all alone, it's riding wide and handsome but it's riding all alone, nobody can use it, perhaps pretty soon we cant use it, it's a mighty lonesome dollar. What you mean, said Fred, what you mean I had some cognac and I dont see what you mean. I mean, said Donald Paul, that our lovely lively dollar is a very lonesome dollar and it lives all alone, alone alone alone, and if you live all alone you get to be kind of lonesome, and if you get kind of lonesome you get to be no good and if you get to be no good, you go kind of bad and if you get kind of bad you dont get at all, and if you dont get you havent got, and where are you, nowhere are you. I tell you our fine dollar is just lonesome. Oh get the hell out of here, said Willie. Yeah, said Jo, the worst of everything is it always sounds as if it was true. Well something has got to be true, said Jimmie. Does it, said Jo, I wonder, well anyway when we get home we wont talk any more not any of us will talk any more and so we wont have to worry whether anything is true or whether it aint true. If you think talking or not makes it different you better think again, said Jimmie, if you think we'll have more chickens or the dollar will buy more just because we get like all those at home and dont talk about it if you think it changes the facts you just better think again. All I know, said Fred, all I know is that they do give you a drink and they dont charge you more for it than they charge a lousy foreign girl who has one. No, said Willie, over there they charge the lousy foreign girl the extra ten cents. I dont believe, said Fred that anybody would do that at home, I dont believe anybody would, I dont believe it. You dont, said Willie, you talk like that when you get back and then they wont give you another drink they'll say you're drunk. Here we are, said Janet, we heard you, tell me something I always wanted to know why do men get so proud of being drunk, anybody can drink, what is it makes men so proud that they can get drunk, there is nothing special about it they all get drunk just exactly the same way, nothing seems any kind of way different but they all each one of 'em are so proud of being drunk. Aint that, said Jo, the way with any vice, cant you say the same about women, any man can sleep with a woman but every man is kind of special proud of it just the same, makes him feel a he-man, yes but about women, said Pauline, some men make women want to more than others. Yes they do, said Willie, yes they do. Oh, said Pauline, what I mean. Yes that is what we do mean, said Willie, No about being drunk. Oh let's forget about being drunk, said Willie, there is only one guy here who can never forget about being drunk and his name is Fred, and he just dont count. Let's talk about women, said Willie. Let's not, said Pauline, let's not, oh dear, said Pauline, when I think again and again about everything I could just cry. It's just as easy not to cry, said Willie, I know it is, said Pauline, that's the reason I am going to cry. How come, said Willie. Where is the man who talks, said Pauline. They wont let him talk any more, said Willie. Who wont let him talk any more, said Janet, the officers. Oh dear no, said Willie, it's all the guys, they found out from listening to him how to do it and now they all talk and talk and think it sounds just like him. And does it, said Pauline. How can I tell, said Willie, I dont listen to them. But you listened to him, said Pauline. Oh yes, said Willie, I listened to him.

Eighteen

I BEEN THINKING, said Brewsie, do we feel alike as well as say alike, do we think alike or dont we think at all. I dont think, said Brewsie, that we feel alike, I think we dont feel alike at all, they say we are sad and I think we are sad because we have different feelings but we articulate all the same. Listen, said Brewsie, you see, said Brewsie, you see I dont think we think, if we thought we could not articulate the same, we couldn't have Gallup polls and have everybody answer yes or no, if you think it's more complicated than that, over here, they wont answer the questions like that, they wont tell you how they are going to think tomorrow but we always know how we gonna think tomorrow because we are all going to think alike, no, said Brewsie, no not think, we are all going to articulate alike, not think, thinking is funnier and more mixed than that, not articulate alike, they ask us

G.I.s what we think about Germans yes or no, my gracious, said Brewsie, you cant just think yes or no about Germans or about Russians and yet we all articulate alike about Germans and Russians, just as if it was the Democratic or Republican Party and it isnt, Willie it isnt, it may be life and death to us and we cant all feel alike and we dont think, is it we cant think, is it that we can only articulate, and if you can only articulate and not think, feel different but no way to get it out, because it comes out and it just is a Gallup poll, yes or no, just like that, oh Willie, I get so worried, I know it is just the most dangerous moment in our history, in a kind of a way as dangerous more dangerous than the Civil War, well they didnt all think alike then, they had lots of complications, and they did think, think how they orated, they did think, and then, said Brewsie, the Civil War was over, and everybody stopped thinking and they began to articulate, and instead of that they became job-hunters, and they felt different all the time they were feeling different, but they were beginning to articulate alike, I guess job men just have to articulate alike, they got to articulate yes or no to their bosses, and yes or no to their unions, they just got to articulate alike, and when you begin to articulate alike, you got to drop thinking out, just got to drop it out, you can go on feeling different but you got to articulate the same Gallup poll, yes you do, and it aint no use making it a second ballot, because nobody can think, how can you think when you feel different, you gotta feel different, anybody does have to feel different, but how can you think when you got to articulate alike. Listen to me Willie, listen to me, it's just like that Willie it just is, said Brewsie. I know, said Willie, it's all right, Brewsie, you got it right it's just the way we are, it's just the way it is, but what are you going to do about it Brewsie. Well that's just it, I kind of think, well I kind of feel that our generation, the generation that saw the depression, the generation that saw the war. I did more than see the depression Brewsie, and I did more than see the war, dont you make no mistake about that Brewsie, I did more than see the depression and I did more than see the war. I know Willie, said Brewsie, I know, I know Willie, and there it is, there was the depression and there was the war, yes but back of that, there is job-mindedness, and what can we do about it. No use saying communism communism, it's stimulating to Russians, because they discovered it, but it wouldnt stimulate us any not any at all. No, said Willie, it certainly would not stimulate me. No I know Willie, said Brewsie, no I just know just how it wouldnt stimulate you but Willie, what we gonna do, we got to think, and how can we think when we got to jump from feeling different to articulating the same, and if we could think Willie what could we think. But, said Willie, Brewsie you just got to hold out some hope, you just got to hold it out. That's very easy to say, said Brewsie, but how can you hold out hope, until you got hope and how can you get hope unless you can think and how can you think when you got to go right from feeling inside you kind of queer and worried and kind of scared and knowing something ought to be done about it articulating all the same thing every minute they ask you something and every minute you open your mouth even when nobody has asked you anything. They talk about cognac, they talk about wine and women, and even that they say just exactly alike, you know it Willie, you know it. Sure I know it Brewsie, sure I know it, but just all the same Brewsie you got to hold out some kind of hope you just got to Brewsie. Well, Willie, I have got some kind of hope not really got it, but it's kind of there and that is because all of us, yes all of us, yes we kind of learned something from suffering, we learned to feel and to feel different and even when it comes to think well we aint learned to think but we kind of learned that if we could think we might think and perhaps if we did not articulate all alike perhaps something might happen. But, said Willie, how about all that job-mindedness, Brewsie, yes, said Willie, how can you not be job-minded when you all have to look for jobs and either get a job or not get a job but you have to do all the time with jobs, how can you be not job-minded if you dont do anything but breathe in a job, think Brewsie, answer me that, said Willie. Yes, said Brewsie, yes sometimes, said Brewsie, when I know how they all feel. They all feel all right they do all feel, said Willie, they do all feel. Well, said Brewsie, when I see how they all feel, sometimes I almost see something. Well look Brewsie look, look all you can Brewsie, and I'll listen while you are looking Brewsie, count on me I told that Pauline I listened to you and I'll listen to you Brewsie I'll listen.

Nineteen

WELL BREWSIE, said Willie, we got 'em, the order has come. Yes I know, said Brewsie. Hullo Jo, said Willie, we got 'em. Sure we got 'em, said Jo. Hullo Willie, said Jimmie. Hullo, said Willie, we got 'em we got orders, we are the boys who are redeployed, in a little boat, on a little shore, and no more will we see a whore whenever we are wherever we are, away so far, it makes me feel funny, kind of funny very funny but it's all right there wont be any thinking over there, no thinking over there, no whores, no thinking, yes Brewsie, nothing but jobs, well do we like it. Yes do we like it, Brewsie, yes do we like it. Well, said John, I am staying, I got no points, so I'll think, do any of you guys want me to think for you. I'll have lots of time, Willie how about you, shall I think the thinks for you. You can stink the stinks for me, but think, well I was gonna say never again, never any thinking, but

I dunno, I kind of think I am going to miss thinking, there was that cute Pauline and there was
thinking, I kind of think I am going to miss thinking, there'll be no thinking over there, they dont
think over there, they got no time to think, they
got to get a job, they got to hold the job, they got
no time to think over there, yes sometimes I might
be kind of lonesome for thinking and I'll be thinking here is John he's got nothing to do, he's having
a hell of a good time just thinking. Yes, said
Brewsie, yes and yes, and dont you think it was
true all we thought over here. Yes, said Willie, of
course it was true but it dont do no good, it dont
help any, it dont, what we gonna do thinking,
what we gonna do. Well I tell you Willie, and if
you dont think a little and go on thinking you'll
have another awful time. Listen Willie, listen,
listen Willie, what's a job, you havent got it,
what's a job, you have got it, what's rushing
around so fast you cant hear yourself think, what
will happen, you'll be old and you never lived, and
you kind of feel silly to lie down and die and to
never have lived, to have been a job chaser and
never have lived. Yes, said Willie, but Brewsie,
now honest to God Brewsie, honest to God and it's
the last time we all are here, honest to God
Brewsie, can you be a job chaser and live at the

same time, honest to God Brewsie tell me that can you live and be a job chaser at the same time, honest to God, Brewsie tell me it, honest to God Brewsie, honest to God. Honest to God Willie, said Brewsie, I just dont know, I just dont know. And if you dont know, said Willie, honest to God who does know. Well, said Jo, I know. What do you know, said Willie. Well, said Jo, I know I am going to. Going to what, said Willie. Honest to God I dont know, said Jo. Well I know, said Jimmie, I dont have to chase jobs, yeah, said Jimmie, because I live in a part of the South where they all live so simple they just cant starve and they live so simple that there aint really much difference between having a job and not having a job, between earning a living and not earning a living, just like these lousy foreigners, said Willie. Well yes perhaps, said Jimmie. And do you think living that way, said Willie. Well, said Jimmie, not so much no and not so much yes, but yes kind of, anyway we can do something that you job chasers cant do, we can listen when other people think and we can sit and wait for them to go on thinking, that's more than you job chasers can do, believe me Willie it's so. Yes, said Willie, I dont say no, yes I know it's so. And said Jo, I know a fellow he is going home to be a bar-keep, he and his brother always wanted to be bar-keeps, and their father never would buy them a bar, and now his brother has been killed in the Pacific and so his father has bought him a bar and is keeping it himself till his son gets home, and the son my God he is fuddled all the time, he is pale and drunk, drunk and pale, my God, said Jo. Well what has that to do with what we got to do, said Jo. Nothing, said Jo, it's just a story. Here we are, said Janet, we heard your crowd were leaving and we came to say good-bye. Good-bye it is sister, said Willie, where is Pauline. She is coming, she said, she wanted to stop and pick you a flower. God bless her for that tender thought, said Willie, God bless her. Yes, said Jo, yes. And said Jimmie, how old is she. What do you want to know that for, said Janet. I just want to know, said Jimmie, if she was her age. Well she aint, said Willie, she's my age. Dear dear, said Janet, isnt that chivalrous unless you are too old. Not so old as that sister, said Willie. And tell me, said Janet, wont you miss talking when you get home, you do know dont you all of you nobody talks like you boys were always talking, not back home. Yes we know, said Jo. Yes we know, said Jimmie. Not Brewsie, said Willie, he'll talk but, said Willie, Brewsie will talk but we wont be there to listen, we kind of will re-

member that he's talking somewhere but we wont
be there to listen, there wont be anybody talking
where we will be. But, said Jo, perhaps they will
talk now, why you all so sure they wont talk over
there, perhaps they will talk over there. Not those
on the job they wont, said Willie. not those on
the job.

To Americans

G.I.s AND G.I.s AND G.I.s and they have made me
come all over patriotic. I was always patriotic, I
was always in my way a Civil War veteran, but in
between, there were other things, but now there
are no other things. And I am sure that this par-
ticular moment in our history is more important
than anything since the Civil War. We are there
where we have to have to fight a spiritual pioneer
fight or we will go poor as England and other industrial countries have gone poor, and dont think
that communism or socialism will save you, you
just have to find a new way, you have to find out
how you can go ahead without running away with
yourselves, you have to learn to produce without
exhausting your country's wealth, you have to
learn to be individual and not just mass job
workers, you have to get courage enough to know
what you feel and not just all be yes or no men, but

you have to really learn to express complication, go easy and if you cant go easy go as easy as you can. Remember the depression, dont be afraid to look it in the face and find out the reason why, dont be afraid of the reason why, if you dont find out the reason why you'll go poor and my God how I would hate to have my native land go poor. Find out the reason why, look facts in the face, not just what they all say, the leaders, but every darn one of you so that a government by the people for the people shall not perish from the face of the earth, it wont, somebody else will do it if we lie down on the job, but of all things dont stop, find out the reason why of the depression, find it out each and every one of you and then look the facts in the face. We are Americans.

ALBERTSON COLLEGE OF IDAHO
PS3537.T323.B7
Brewsie and Willie.

3 5556 00039751 3

DATE DUE

PRINTED IN U.S.A.